Builder

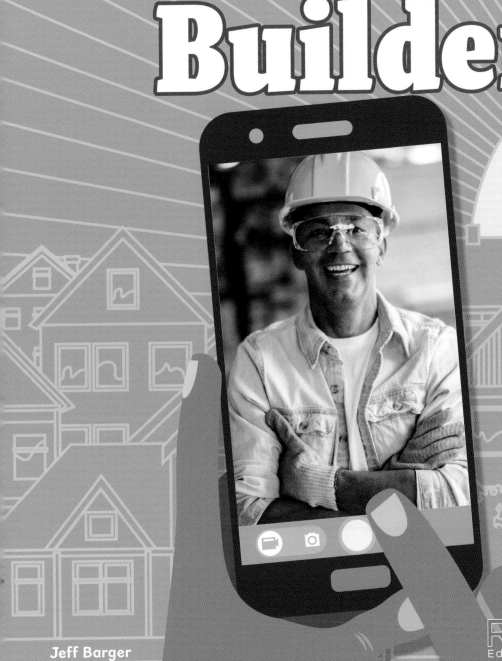

Jeff Barger

Educational Media
rourkeeducationalmedia.com

A Division of
Carson Dellosa Education

T0014712

BEFORE AND DURING READING ACTIVITIES

Before Reading: *Building Background Knowledge and Vocabulary*

Building background knowledge can help children process new information and build upon what they already know. Before reading a book, it is important to tap into what children already know about the topic. This will help them develop their vocabulary and increase their reading comprehension.

Questions and Activities to Build Background Knowledge:

1. Look at the front cover of the book and read the title. What do you think this book will be about?
2. What do you already know about this topic?
3. Take a book walk and skim the pages. Look at the table of contents, photographs, captions, and bold words. Did these text features give you any information or predictions about what you will read in this book?

Vocabulary: *Vocabulary Is Key to Reading Comprehension*

Use the following directions to prompt a conversation about each word.

- Read the vocabulary words.
- What comes to mind when you see each word?
- What do you think each word means?

Vocabulary Words:
- *construct*
- *frame*
- *shelter*
- *site*

During Reading: *Reading for Meaning and Understanding*

To achieve deep comprehension of a book, children are encouraged to use close reading strategies. During reading, it is important to have children stop and make connections. These connections result in deeper analysis and understanding of a book.

Close Reading a Text

During reading, have children stop and talk about the following:

- Any confusing parts
- Any unknown words
- Text to text, text to self, text to world connections
- The main idea in each chapter or heading

Encourage children to use context clues to determine the meaning of any unknown words. These strategies will help children learn to analyze the text more thoroughly as they read.

When you are finished reading this book, turn to the next-to-last page for an *After Reading Activity*.

Table of Contents

Community Helpers

Community helpers are all around us. They make our lives better.

People who live or work in the same area are part of a community.

Builders are community helpers.

Builders **construct** buildings.

Plans for building a house are called blueprints.

Types of Buildings

Some workers build hospitals.

Some workers build schools.

Many schools are built with bricks.

Some build houses.

Some build skyscrapers.

A scaffold lets builders work in high places.

On the Job

A builder works on a construction **site**.

The lead builder is called a foreman.

They use special tools.

Safety is important. Construction tools can cause injuries.

Some builders cut wood with saws.
Others **frame** buildings with steel.

Workers wear hard hats to protect their heads.

Buildings give us **shelter**.

Buildings keep us safe.

A new home is an exciting place!

Builders build places for us to live, work, and play.

They are important community helpers.

Activity

Build a Community

Supplies

- empty boxes (cereal boxes, shoeboxes, or others)
- scissors
- construction paper
- glue or tape
- crayons
- markers

Directions

1. You are building a new community. What buildings do you need? Choose five to start with.
2. Select one or more empty boxes to use for each building. Ask an adult to help you cut doors and windows.
3. Cut paper to cover each building. Tape or glue it in place.
4. Use crayons or markers to decorate the buildings and make them look real.
5. Arrange your buildings in a community.

Photo Glossary

 **construct** (kuhn-STRUHKT): To make or build something.

 **frame** (frame): To make the basic structure that provides the support for a building.

 **shelter** (SHEL-tur): A place that offers protection from bad weather or danger.

 **site** (site): The place where something is located or where something is happening.

Index

After Reading Activity

What building would you like to add to your community? Draw a picture of what it would look like. Write a name for your building and describe what you might find inside.

About the Author

Jeff Barger is an author, blogger, and literacy specialist. He lives in North Carolina. He can build a sandwich and that's about it. His favorite building is a skyscraper.

www.rourkeeducationalmedia.com

Edited by: Kim Thompson
Cover and interior design by: Kathy Walsh

Photo Credits: Cover, title page, p.20: ©andresr; p.5: ©Rawpixel.com; p.7, 22: ©Justin Horrocks; p.9: ©BrianGuest; p.11: ©ewg3D; p.13, 22: ©Steve Debenport; p.15: ©TommL; p.17, 22: ©sturti; p.19, 22: ©monkeybusinessimages

Library of Congress PCN Data

Builder / Jeff Barger
(Community Helpers)
ISBN 978-1-73161-424-7 (hard cover)(alk. paper)
ISBN 978-1-73161-219-9 (soft cover)
ISBN 978-1-73161-529-9 (e-Book)
ISBN 978-1-73161-634-0 (ePub)
Library of Congress Control Number: 2019932041

Rourke Educational Media
Printed in the United States of America,
North Mankato, Minnesota